A QUICK GUIDE

TO WINNING

WRITING CONTESTS

by Patricia La Barbera

CONTENTS

Introduction

Congratulations! By reading this book, you're taking a step toward winning a writing contest.

But why enter writing contests?

In addition to the obvious monetary benefits associated with winning some competitions, other advantages include the potential for editors, publishers, and other influential people to notice your work. And even if you *only* make the honorable-mention list, it's still publicity.

Prizes vary from none to thousands of dollars. Sometimes writers compete for a free edit from the judge or even a publishing contract. Entering contests also provides incentives to write.

The Publishing Contest

Don't writers win contests every time they're published?

Definitely.

Writers compete against a slush-pile mountain, and this book benefits many fiction authors, especially those writing in genre categories.

Another Contest

Which book will a person buy? Although many elements can influence purchasing decisions, an attention-getting title and a riveting sample excerpt might clinch a sale.

I've judged thousands of contest entries. It always amazes me that opportunities for significant improvement fall into categories that many writers either don't know about or ignore. For example, about 90 percent of the stories I read would benefit from improving one of the following: title, beginning hook, or ending. In all three categories, revision could benefit at least 50 percent.

As you read this book, you should recognize some areas for your own work's improvement. Zero in on those subjects first, rather than have the material overwhelm you. I dedicated my book *Genre Writing* to "beginning writers who feel like avalanche victims." I remember how I felt when I first started writing.

Although this book targets genre categories, it can also benefit those who write literary fiction.

The topics discussed give people an edge over uninformed contestants. Learn the conventions that will separate amateurs from professionals and increase a judge's interest.

Don't bore the judge, especially in the first few paragraphs. Discover five things the beginning should have and elements that are not as effective.

Ignoring certain requirements might put you at a disadvantage or possibly disqualify your entry. One chapter reveals details about contest prompts. Another covers common entry mistakes.

How many people research contest judges? This guide offers suggestions on gathering information.

Few things are more of a letdown than reading a story that's fantastic only to reach an ending that fizzles. Discover finales that work and those that are not as satisfying.

One of the most important chapters offers a concise summary of elements that may cause your entry's rise to the top of the pile.

Don't waste time and money entering contests without preparation. This book's information might tip the scales in your favor.

I didn't intend to offer exhaustive topic discussions. Instead, I'm presenting important elements of a prize-worthy contest entry. If you're interested in expanding your understanding of any topics, I'd suggest searching the Writer's Knowledge Base, which you can find at https://hiveword.com/wkb/search. Unlike generic search engines that require wading through lists of irrelevant internet addresses, this resource yields only handpicked writer-specific sites.

Relax. There's no test at the end, and no math will haunt you. I've tried to keep things concise and informal. I've also tried to inject humor. Winning writing contests is serious business, but when you're reading about them, there's no rule that says you can't smile.

Be careful, though, that you don't read more about writing than you actually write. Curb this behavior by joining critique groups, either those that meet in person or online. As another incentive, decide on a schedule to submit stories to magazines and contests. Duotrope.com is a valuable resource for finding markets.

In case you're wondering (or worrying), I haven't used anyone else's writing but my own to illustrate good or bad examples.

Disclaimer: I can't guarantee that by reading this book, you'll win a writing contest. Ideas expressed in this book are my opinions and may not reflect the views and assessments of your story's judge.

1

First Advice

Everyone knows you leave only one space between sentences, right?

Wrong, based on the evidence. Leaving two spaces between sentences used to be the norm, but if you continue the practice, people will wonder what rock you've just crawled out from under.

Does that sound harsh? Maybe so, but don't have your judge start out with a bad impression. There's nothing wrong with being a beginning writer, but it's no one's business.

But There Are No Rules!

Well, writing *conventions* exist, and I'll cover many of them. However, if any interfere with what you really feel is the best way to tell your story, ignore them. Make sure, though, you don't disregard conventions just to be a rebel—not until you're rich and famous anyway.

Contests usually do have *rules* about manuscript formatting. Break those at your own risk.

Avoid including the following items unless the contest rules state they're acceptable:

- a frame on any page
- any font color other than black
- family crests
- character illustrations
- graphics (especially animations)
- photographs
- distracting scene-break indicators

If you include the above items, you may as well type the byline as "by (author's name), amateur."

Some competitions have required subjects and perhaps various other prompts. To avoid disqualification, make sure your story contains the necessary elements.

2

Judges

There's no reason to enter writing contests if you don't want money, fame, and promotion.

Seriously, opportunities abound for writers when they enter contests.

Besides the obvious monetary goals associated with winning some competitions, an additional advantage for successful competitors includes the possibility of attention from judges, who may be editors, publishers, or other influential people. Even if you *only* make the honorable-mention list, it's still publicity.

Prizes can vary from none to thousands of dollars. At times, writers compete for a free edit or even a publishing contract. Some people use contests as an incentive to write.

If the contest reveals who the judge is, attempt to learn his likes and dislikes. Often an internet search will yield this information.

Many judges are magazine editors and may give interviews. Discover valuable data by consulting sources, such as Duotrope, that interview publishers and by reading the submission guidelines of the judge's magazine.

Judges from all categories, whether writers, editors, or publishers, often have strong likes and dislikes. If you can't find information about the judge, consider avoiding some of the frequently mentioned things that annoy people. The next section, as well as the rest of the book, reveals some of the riskier elements.

When you're choosing which writing contests to enter, consider selecting those whose judges provide feedback. Even if you don't win, the remarks can guide your revision.

Tails Tales: A Talk on the Wild Side

Some people have negative feelings about a story whose protagonist is an animal, especially a talking animal. I've read some good stories with animals as main characters and some terrible ones. Maybe your story is great. Perhaps you'll be fortunate enough to get a judge who tolerates or even loves stories that have animal protagonists. Consider, though, if it's in your best interest to submit something whose favorable reception is iffy.

This situation is an example of when researching the judge is beneficial. And while we're on the subject of animals, don't include any cruelty to them. This also applies to children. Many contests won't tolerate graphic violence involving any kind of victim.

Unintentional Offense

You don't have to be on a soapbox via your characters to irritate a reader. An audience might misconstrue something that the writer expresses. For example, in my book *The Celtic Crow Murders*, the protagonist goes fishing with her father and daughter and catches dolphin. Later they eat them for dinner. Someone critiquing the story before publication expressed horror that I'd have my main character catching and eating those adorable performing mammals. I revised the scene so it would be unmistakable that the characters caught the fish variety of dolphin.

Other things about characters that might upset readers include their wearing animal fur or driving a gas-guzzler.

Point of View on a Point of View

Second-person point of view (You walk to the library and . . .) doesn't have universal appeal, so you might consider this when choosing the story's point of view.

3

Prompts

A positive aspect of writing contests with prompts is that they provide a structure for a story, which some contestants prefer. Musing on things such as a required setting, genre, object, character, time period, or conflict often sparks creativity.

The challenge with prompts is that a writer must know how strictly he has to follow them. *Unless specifically stated otherwise in the rules of the competition*, using the prompt in a straightforward way is a good idea.

In other words, don't get fancy, unless the contest rules say you can. If an *object* prompt is a flower that *must be* an integral part of the story or just appear in the story once, be sure to use the word *flower* as a noun, not as a verb. And use the word *flower* at least once, even if you also use the name of the kind of flower it is. Don't use it as an acronym either. Don't use it as someone's name and think you've met the obligation of the prompt. Not using the object prompt or any other prompt or not using it properly will put you at risk for disqualification or losing points.

Don't try to force the prompts into a prewritten story, especially if doing so is against the contest rules. Often the revision isn't smooth and therefore not successful.

Be leery of submitting an excerpt from your WIP (work in progress) book even if it meets the prompt requirements and the contest's other rules unless it has a strong story arc. Without the story arc, the piece is a slice-of-life story, also known as a vignette. Some stories that I suspect writers lifted from a longer work either end too abruptly or just fade away without any sense of resolution.

4

To Plot or Not

I'll bet you thought I'd start with the title. No, it's fine to grab on to any title because you have to save the file. Many compelling titles reveal themselves during the writing process.

So, here's the scenario. You're sitting in front of your computer and feel blindfolded as you try to whack the heck out of the plot piñata. Don't, unless you're convinced that out of the two, plotters or pantsers (who write by the seat of their pants), you're one of the former. I'd be the last person to try to convince you otherwise, but I've read some information on plotting that's so intricate and formulaic that it sounds like geometry.

I don't know about you, but I got involved with writing because I'd heard there'd be no math. And in the introduction, I said there'd be none of that. However, if you do consider yourself a plotter, I won't talk you out of it. If you're happy with the results, then great.

Both plotters and pantsers have to start with a story idea. But pantsers don't have to think up the whole enchilada right away.

Fishing for Story Ideas

The words *mind numbing* describe how many ways you can discover story ideas. Consider the following suggestions:

- **Expand upon or exaggerate a travel experience.** Imagine the opposite of how the trip went. Raise the stakes about getting there or getting back. Have the protagonist get lost, robbed, arrested, or abducted. Turn the story into a mystery, horror, or romance tale. Add paranormal elements, mistaken identity, amnesia, a crumbling mansion, a deserted island. Caution—probably not all of these in one story, although it would be an interesting challenge.

- **Scan the dictionary until you find a word that fascinates you.** I've used this technique several times. If you don't get an idea right away, record the word in a notebook. You'll be surprised (and maybe disturbed) at the ideas one word can generate.
- **Read the newspaper for creative inspiration.** No doubt, you will feel a powerful impetus drawing you to the safety and consolation of your bed. Resistance is not futile. Use those sensational, depressing, violent, or oddball gems in your masterpiece.
- **Eavesdrop on a bus or subway.** If you're sitting near a loudmouth, you're a captive audience anyway.
- **Ask a taxi driver about the weirdest passenger.** Try to prepare yourself for the answer, and remember to breathe.
- **Listen in on a restaurant conversation.** Position yourself near people who are

sneering, shouting, or weeping. Accrue one hundred extra points if diners throw food or drinks at each other. Double it if they hit you.

- **Attend a trial.** Try to concentrate, even though you're embarrassed because you feel none of it is any of your business.

- **Visit a museum and note the people, the art, and the comments.** Plan this field trip for when the place is crowded, and wear sunglasses and a floppy hat. Carry a cane topped with a carved fantastical beast. No one will pay any attention to you. You will be invisible. You are in an art museum.

- **Scan a phonebook for interesting names you can tweak and use in your tale.** Do this only when you're not in a rush because of all the time wasted by hilarity.

- **Promise yourself you'll write a story about the first product you see when you open a catalogue.** Be careful what catalogue you open.

- **Visit an old cemetery and read gravestones.** Try not to attract attention. Try not to think about how your being alive makes you outnumbered. Feel free to plan the quickest escape route.

- **Browse the Internet or read the newspaper.** Use this option only if you're in the mood for story-idea overload.

If you're fortunate enough to know who'll be judging your story, researching the types of writing and the subjects he or she likes is well worth the effort. Taking into account the preferences of the contest's sponsor may also give you some guidance.

Be sure to keep a small notebook with you at all times so you can record writing-related inspirations

I mulled over adding the following thoughts, and I have to admit they're subjective. I don't think it's a good idea to sit in front of a computer if you have absolutely no story ideas. It usually results in weeping, gnashing of teeth, and high blood pressure.

When you have some inspiration, write as much as you can. Don't worry if there's not much on the page or if it's just a list. Don't bother to self-edit. Especially don't obsess over the fact that you don't know how the story will end.

Write until you've run out of ideas, and then put it aside and get involved in something else. It's amazing how quickly you'll think about ways of developing whatever you wrote. Even if you don't have an aha moment soon, it will be worth it to let those ideas percolate.

Here's the good news: once you start down the path of finding story ideas, they'll start finding you.

5

The Plot Quickens

I'm not sure why, but I'm commenting more about plot weakness. Plot-anemic writing, no matter how ethereal and literary the prose, is the *kiss of debt* for commercial fiction writers.

What is the barebones description of a plot? Someone wants something and faces challenges to get it. The main character may or may not get what she wants, but the story should include some kind of change in at least the protagonist, perhaps other characters, and possibly the situation.

A Plot Is Not . . .

I've read stories in which almost nothing happens. The author describes the setting in vivid and poetic terms. The prose is solid. The reader might learn something about the three-dimensional main character's interesting backstory. But there's no tangible challenge, the character doesn't seem to strive for anything, and there's no real change with the protagonist, other characters, or the situation. If there's no conflict or change, there's no story.

Sometimes the protagonist's efforts at reaching a goal are so minimal that either she doesn't get what she wants or she reaches her goal by something that isn't attributable to her.

Besides decreasing a reader's involvement, the previous scenarios interfere with constructing an ending that has a satisfying sense of resolution and that resonates.

Let's assume you're trying to plot a story idea where the main character, the protagonist, needs to find the villain, the antagonist, who kidnapped his daughter. The story has a built-in suspense factor. Although the stakes are already high, you could raise them by having the criminal issue a terrifying ultimatum about what he'll do if the man goes to the police or doesn't give him the ransom money.

I'll admit this story idea isn't original. Be leery about using the first story idea that pops into your head. It's likely to have popped into many heads. How could you make the plot more interesting?

Consider the following plot twists:

- The kidnapper might demand a ransom that's more difficult to get than money. He might ask the father to kill someone, steal something, or decipher a code.
- The man who thinks he's her father isn't, and he's abusing her. Her biological father kidnaps her to get her away from the man who's abusing her.
- The father pays the ransom money and the kidnapper returns the child, but the child turns out to be a realistic robot, which the father may or may not realize.

- The government is kidnapping children to colonize another planet or a remote place on earth.

A Few More Things about Plots

Be careful your plot isn't too ambitious for a short story, especially for flash fiction. If you could capsulize a description into something like this—the saga of a family's Conestoga-wagon journey from Maine to California—alarm bells should blare. Writing about an episode during the grueling trip is possible, though.

In the horror genre, I've read stories with much carnage, but no plot development or sense of resolution. Buckets of blood won't help a non-plot, no matter how enthusiastically the author splashes them around.

As mentioned previously, don't think you can pluck several pages from your work in progress and pass it off as a freestanding story unless it has the elements of one. And strong indications that the author may have lifted the piece from a WIP, other than a plot so weak that the story reads like a vignette, are unexplained people, things, or situations and an abrupt ending with poor or absent resolution.

6

First Paragraph,
Not Worst Paragraph

A first paragraph controls a story's life or death. Maybe I sound dramatic, but it's true that many readers, including some acquisition editors, will stop reading if they don't like a story's beginning.

In my role as a contest judge, I always read the entire story, but a weak beginning has a negative effect. A poor start doesn't evoke a strong desire to continue reading. It doesn't elicit curiosity or intrigue.

Experienced writers know how important it is for the beginning to capture the reader's interest.

When a story has a bland start, it suggests the writer is an amateur. Entries that I give the highest scores to usually have exceptional beginnings and display excellence throughout the piece.

I hope I've convinced you about the importance of your story's beginning. But what are some ways of starting a story that usually aren't in your best interest?

Backstory

I was born in a small Midwestern town in the second half of the twentieth century. Our town was like most others in the state. We had a Main Street, one hotel with a fine restaurant, and two gas stations that sold coffee and homemade donuts.

Mr. Stevens ran the pharmacy, the kind with a counter and stools. If I close my eyes, I can see that store and taste that ice-cold sarsaparilla. Life there wasn't exciting, but we had the best high school football team, and . . .

Are you asleep yet?

Start the story where the story starts—in the immediacy of a scene. In many stories with beginning narrative, there's a point after a few paragraphs that's a great place to start and provides a compelling beginning sentence. You can weave in the *important* information rather than having it blitz the reader.

Talking Heads in White Space

"I'm glad to see you."

"It's been a while."

"Sure has."

"You know, I was wondering about something."

"What?"

"Well, you know that thing we were talking about on the phone."

"Yeah. What about it?"

"I still don't think we should go to that first place."

"So, you think the second place we talked about would be better?"

"Yeah, and I'm sure you know why."

"Yeah."

Okay, I'm exaggerating a little with this dialogue, but I don't know who these people are. I don't know what their relationship is. I don't know why they're talking to each other. I don't know where they're talking to each other. I don't know where the first place is. I don't know why the second place is better. I don't know why . . .

This type of beginning doesn't evoke intrigue or curiosity. It creates mystification and irritation.

The next example concerns a beginning paragraph's length, and it is the *unparagraphed* version of the beginning of my book *Castle Wolves*.

Long First Paragraph

Had the crown prince given her a piercing glance? Lady Merewyn tried not to roll her eyes. Yes, she was sure he had because now Prince Alexander stared at her from the royal dining table. If only the insufferable spoiled brat would just keep his eyes to himself. He was even more annoying than when they were children. Of course, he wanted anyone to notice him, even her. His younger brother, Thomas, had everyone's attention because of his tunic ceremony. She breathed a big sigh. Prince Alexander was making her more irritable than usual. Her father glared and leaned toward her ear. "If you start . . ." She gave him a sidelong glance but kept her lips closed. Merewyn felt the smooth crimson tablecloth and then ran her finger over an embroidered golden bird in flight. If only she were that bird. Merewyn touched her forehead—warm. Had the fever returned? She hoped not. The evening would be difficult enough without her being ill. The king rose and bowed to the priest. "On this solemn and joyous occasion, I ask you, Father, to lead us in prayer." Solemn *and* joyous?

Merewyn winced. Only a king could say that. The priest stood and signaled for everyone to rise. "Let us thank the Trinity—God the Father, God the Son, and God the Holy Spirit—for all of our blessings and ask special ones for Prince Thomas." He faced the prince. "Always ask God the Father for protection through God the Son, Our Lord Jesus Christ." The priest led the crowd in the Our Father and the prayer before a meal. After the prayers, the king thanked the priest and sat down. The guests continued with their merry chatter. Prince Alexander stood.

If you read the entire excerpt, you deserve a medal. With a paragraph this long, it doesn't matter what the content is. I *have* read manuscripts with full-page first paragraphs. I think it's obvious why long paragraphs aren't a good idea for the beginning, middle, or end. I'll cover more about this topic in a later section.

Are you still reading? Yes? Great! Here's another example of a bad first paragraph and a little of what follows:

Incongruous First Sentence

A bloody severed arm stained the sink bright red. Farnsworth blinked, and it disappeared. "I must be crazy to imagine that," he said, though he was the only person in the bathroom. "I'm probably not getting enough sleep."

"Honey, the waffles are getting cold," his wife yelled. "And I don't want you to be late for your job interview."

So what's wrong with this?

Tacking on a grotesque first sentence that has nothing to do with the story is a cheap trick. Of course, you don't know it has nothing to do with the story. You'll just have to take my word for it.

And you don't want to risk annoying horror readers either, do you? I didn't think so.

The next story's problem beginning involves description.

An Upsetting Setting

An ancient weather-beaten barn stood proudly in the primeval cleft of the sublime mountain slopes. The mighty sun stretched its piercing rays in anticipation of its hard-earned nightly respite, and fully flooded the late and lazy afternoon with a purplish miasma. Piebald baby goats danced an effervescent jig of exuberance to the soporific drone of their winged insect companions. Long ago, the moist dew on the bucolic meadow had vanished, and the warty frogs croaked out their funereal dirge with brio. Now, a light zephyr pirouetted intermittently through the pristine meadow, causing the variegated blossoms to undulate to its mesmerizing rhythms. A battalion of Canadian geese . . .

This is out-of-control description on Spring Break, and it needs handcuffs. I could go on and on with it, and sometimes stories do. Who's the protagonist? Is it the proud ancient barn or perhaps the battalion leader of the Canadian geese? Where are we going with this? And the anthropomorphism is ridiculous. Yes, I know I wrote it. Or was it my evil twin?

Oh, and note the –ly adverbs and the speed-bump adjectives and try not to use them. Ditto with the awkward alliteration. In fact, try to wipe the entire paragraph from your memory.

What is an effective ways to reveal the setting?

An Interacting Character

The storm had caught him, but would the bounty hunter? Wesley stumbled into the weather-beaten barn, and hoped it wouldn't collapse. Rain and sweat had drenched him. He pulled off his red bandana. Wesley pressed it to his lips and stifled a sob. Annie had embroidered their names on it the night before he . . .

In the barn's far reaches, darkness crouched. How did Arizona kill murderers? A rafter held a hooting owl and a frayed rope ending in a noose.

Additional Thoughts on Settings

Reveal the character's state of mind with objects, such as shadows, an unrelenting sun, looming mountains, haunting crows, ominous caws, a trailing mountain lion.

Let details in the setting remind the protagonist of story elements: a rafter, a cloud formation in the shape of a person's face, a rock resembling a tombstone, mourning wind, red earth.

Introduce another character and reveal some description in the dialogue.

Rather than using chunks of description, sprinkle it in.

Have the prose reflect the character's voice, not an external narrator's voice.

Your Cheating Start

Vladimir set his jaw and squared his shoulders. Destiny bellowed its demand. This time he'd accomplish the impossible. Steeling himself against the screeches and roars, he entered the cave's black maw. The walls echoed the diabolic cacophony.

He stopped.

Terror flooded his body. Would fear conquer him again? Vladimir took a deep breath and dragged his feet toward the infernal madness. But the sounds of scraping and dragging approached. Howling and snarls closed in.

A sulfuric stench attacked him. Razor-sharp teeth ripped his chest and—

Vladimir, wheezing, bolted upright. He flung his arm on the nightstand, and clawed for his asthma inhaler.

This is cheating. I think the only things worse than it-was-all-a-dream beginnings are it-was-all-a-dream endings.

The Disappearing Act

The next beginning I like to think of as the disappearing act, and this occurrence is even worse in a novel than in short fiction. Imagine you're reading the beginning of a story, and the writer introduces an exciting scene with an engaging character named Beth. She goes through a high-stress situation. The writer tells the story in the scene through Beth's perspective. Despite her difficulties, Beth manages to save someone's life, and her courageous behavior makes her admirable.

In the next scene, the writer introduces a man named Gary, who's also an appealing character. Gary is the scene's perspective character. He may or may not go through a high-stress situation. The scene ends and the third one begins. Again the perspective character is Gary. By now, the reader may start wondering what happened to Beth. The fourth scene begins, and it turns out that Gary is in the starring role here, too. Now the reader *really* may be wondering what happened to Beth.

In some stories this very interesting first character is never mentioned again, but the reader has been prepped to believe the person will be pivotal. The reader's wondering what happened to Beth may detract from his concentration on the story because in the back of his mind, her fate is a running question.

How do you fix something like this?

I'd suggest that you decide if you need to start with a disposable character and not the story's protagonist or other recurring character. If you don't want to start with the main character or other essential character, then consider not naming the character and not making her three dimensional. If the plot makes her death realistic, then her death would add to the finality of her story involvement.

To draw your reader in, consider including the following items as early as possible, even in the first paragraph, especially for flash fiction:

- Introduce the protagonist by name.

- Reveal the setting. This doesn't have to be elaborate. Just state where the action takes place, for example, an office, a park, or a train. Avoid talking heads in white space.

- Include a hook. Some ideas for good beginning sentences include those containing a question, an intriguing situation, a dilemma, a conflict, or a dangerous element. In other words, something that will catch the reader's interest and evoke curiosity regarding a solution.

- Start to build rapport between readers and the protagonist, which will spark interest and engagement with the character and the story. Identifying the character by name will contribute to audience involvement.

- Reveal the genre.

This may seem formulaic, but it's a guide to what's important to have in a story's beginning, perhaps not all in the first paragraph.

The following paragraph starts my book *The Celtic Crow Murders*. Can you identify the five elements mentioned above?

Aaron's death was no accident. Larissa gripped the edge of her husband's open casket and bit her lip. No matter what the police said. She glanced around the room. All the other mourners had left the funeral home. So why did she feel someone's presence?

The elements are the following items:

- The setting is a funeral home.
- The protagonist is Larissa.
- Building rapport happens by revealing that Larissa is distressed. She's gripping the open casket and biting her lip.
- The hook is she's alone, but senses someone's there.
- The genre is mystery. She thinks Aaron's death wasn't an accident.

7

Pacing and Speed Bumps

I've often read submissions from writers who must have devoted much time and effort to their stories' beginnings because of their high quality. However, after the initial intrigue, the pace starts to drag.

It's always a bad sign when I'm in the middle of reading a contest entry, and I start squirming. Then I get up for a glass of water. Before I return to the computer, I always check on the cat, who's usually sleeping. She usually wakes up and looks at me as though she's asking what. Some days I drink a lot of water. On those days I imagine that if Maeve could talk, she'd tell me to mind my own business.

One reason for my fidgety behavior is a poorly constructed plot. The other culprits are speed bumps.

A speed bump is any story element that causes a distraction. It interferes with the flow and takes the reader out of the story. Speed bumps come in many shapes and sizes, and I'll discuss several.

Catch Your Errors Before Your Reader Does

Elements such as omitted words, misspellings, repeated words, unusual words, awkward rhymes, and excessive alliteration create speed bumps. Tongue twisters are not only hard to say, but they're also hard to read.

A solution to these problems, other than more careful proofreading, is to read the story aloud. Some word-processing programs convert text to speech, and the newer ones have improved voice quality. Using this tool is an effective step in your proofreading strategy.

Story elements that don't seem realistic are distracting. I often comment that something requires suspension of disbelief. This category includes possibilities such as characters doing things that are *out of character* or just don't make sense.

It's better to avoid having characters behave in this fashion, but you may feel the plot requires an inexplicable action. If the character expresses in dialogue or internal dialogue that she knows her behavior doesn't make sense, but gives some kind of excuse for it, the reader might accept it. This suggestion is particularly applicable where unnecessary foolhardy danger is concerned, though you still run the risk of making your character unappealing.

The caveat regarding "things that don't make sense" isn't restricted to characters' behaviors. Any unrealistic element in the plot, setting, or ending can cause head scratching.

And while I'm on the subject of items that require suspension of disbelief, here are some examples of what you would *not* think about while being chased through the forest by giant carnivorous squirrels:

- squirrel evolution
- the effects of logging on the environment
- the best places to buy hiking boots
- fond memories of other camping trips

But it *is* realistic you *would* be thinking of this:

Surviving!

This may seem amusing, but you'd be amazed at what some writers have their characters thinking about while they're running for their lives.

Punctuation Inundation

Punctuation marks are important because they help you maneuver through a sentence. They're like traffic signs. It's to your advantage, though, to have only the essential marks. A punctuation mark creates a pause, however brief.

Excessive or incorrect punctuation interferes with a sentence's flow.

Don't use more than one ending punctuation mark. What am I talking about?!! That.

Appellation Designation

Don't risk confusion by choosing similar names for your characters. In fact, think twice before having characters with the same first initial.

Easier *Said* than Overdone

Stick with *said* for dialogue tags and only use the word when necessary to reveal the speaker. The word is almost invisible because it's so common. Verbs such as *retorted, uttered, announced, responded,* or *recited* jump off the page. Some verbs also don't belong in a dialogue tag because speech is impossible with them. Examples of these verbs include *breathed, laughed, giggled, frowned, chortled, beamed, hiccupped,* and *sighed.* However, you can use them in beats that show action, define the speaker, and reveal details. Be cautious about using the word *gasp* anywhere. It gives some editors hives.

Order in the . . . Dialogue Tag

Use the character's name first rather than *said* as in the following: "Gregory said," not "said Gregory.

Chimerical Creations

A chimera is an imaginary beast made up of incongruous elements. Writers who try to revise is/was/were sentences sometimes wind up with chimerical creations. It's better to have the occasional is/was/were sentence that's transparent and maintains the pace rather than a tortuous construction that brings the head-scratching reader to a halt.

Brick Walls

Speed bumps on steroids or in multitudes are often brick walls. They can have the same effect on readers that brick walls sometimes have on drivers—a complete and final stop.

Logical Chronological

Ping-ponging through your story by jumping back and forth in its history can sometimes create brick walls. I'm not saying it can't be done, but I'd suggest getting a lot of feedback regarding if the transitions are smooth and clear. Otherwise, you run the risk of frustrating and irritating your judge.

8

Titles

I wonder why people choose boring titles. One-word titles underwhelm, especially if the words refer to something abstract, such as love, freedom, hatred, jealousy, or curiosity.

Maybe you don't think titles are that important. I'll be honest with you. Maybe they aren't for some judges, but I think they're essential.

A title that's clever or intriguing puts me in a good mood. It makes me feel that the writer knows what she's doing. I have positive expectations about the story. I'm not saying a title is more important than the other elements, but a title is one of the things that can enhance a contest entry.

How do you create an attention-getting and memorable title?

For example, take the boring, one-word title "Love" and embellish it according to your story content:

Getting Personal

Victoria's Love

The ____ of Love

The Architecture of Love
The Mathematics of Love

Love as an Adjective

The Love Department

Freshening a Phrase

Jung Love
Love Handel
The Funnel of Love

Rhyme

Above Love

Subjects Related to Love

Emotion Sickness

Steeled with a Kiss

Contradiction

Affectionate Enemy

Genre Relevance

Examples of using the word *forest* or *forests* to match some genres follow:

Science fiction: Forests at a Galaxy's Edge

Mystery: Murders in Skull Forest

Fantasy: Arathon's Dream Forest

Horror: Forest of Fear

Romance: The Forest of the Heart

Dynamic with Verbs

Dream in the Arathon Forest

Murders Haunt Skull Forest

Forests Crowd a Galaxy's Edge

Effective Repetition

Decide on a motif phrase or sentence that could have a double meaning, and use it as a title as well as sprinkling it throughout your story as a sentence or fragment paragraph. At the end, use it as your final sentence. This ending is particularly effective if the interpretation of the ending sentence or fragment is different from the meaning of the other sentences or fragments.

The Good News

Don't worry if you're having trouble thinking about a title. As I mentioned earlier, it's fine to grab on to any name because you have to save the file. Many compelling titles reveal themselves during the writing process.

9

The Button Box

One of my fondest childhood memories is my grandmother's button box. Such an amazing hodge-podge of sparkly orbs, golden squares, silver animals, and flowers trapped in acrylic wonder, to name a few. I offer the following assorted elements, though not as fascinating as those in my grandmother's button box, for your perusal.

Emphasis

Avoid emphasizing by bolding, capitalizing, or underlining (or even worse, all three). Use just *italicizing* instead, and use it sparingly. It's usually not advisable to italicize paragraphs. Large blocks of italicized text are distracting and a strain to read.

Don't italicize thoughts. Instead, blending them into the text is the trend, unless the character is addressing someone in her thoughts.

Regardless of the previous advice, you can't imagine how many times while writing this book I've wanted to bold, capitalize, and underline some advice. So far, I've controlled myself.

Punctuation

- Avoid using multiple dashes on a page, and have no more than two in a sentence.
- Don't include parentheses in fiction. They're distracting, and they interfere with the flow.
- Skip semicolons and colons in genre fiction.
- A comma splice is not nice, revise into two sentences. These are two complete sentences, and the comma between them is incorrect punctuation. Revise into two sentences. Another fix is the following: A comma splice is not nice, so revise into two sentences.

Lo-o-o-o-ng Sentences and Paragraphs

Long paragraphs and sentences also make the pace drag. Add interest to the prose with variations in sentence and paragraph lengths.

Break up long, narrative-heavy paragraphs with dialogue and action.

If you have only one character in a scene, the character could talk out loud to himself. He also could say a prayer or speak to an object. The character might talk to another character in his thoughts, and that could create a new paragraph.

Fragments can smooth the prose and add variety. Writing them well usually takes some skill development. It's beneficial to note their use in modern bestsellers to develop an ear for them.

Use one-sentence paragraphs for emphasis and impact.

Add onomatopoeia as a one-word-sentence paragraph.

Start a sentence with a conjunction for emphasis and variety:

"But you didn't, did you?"

Try to Remember

The expression isn't "try and." It's "try to."

Lie/Lay

Lie (*lie, lay, lying*) is intransitive, and it means to recline. (Lie down, Jimmy. Jimmy lay on the sofa. He's been lying there since breakfast.) *Lay* (*lay, laid, laying*) is transitive (takes a direct object) and it means to set something down. (Lay the dish on the counter. She laid the plate down. She's laying the plate down now.)

This issue is confusing for many people, particularly the verb *laid*. Note the example above: <u>Jimmy lay on the sofa</u>, *not* Jimmy laid on the sofa. Yes, I underlined the correct sentence. That's how important it is. However, this sentence would be correct (odd but correct): The chicken laid eggs on the sofa.

Buddy, Could You Spare an Of

I know this relates to idiom, but it grates on my nerves when people write something like "a couple ideas" rather than "a couple of ideas."

Standard Spelling

Use *toward* instead of *towards* and leave the *s* off other similar directional words, such as *forward* and *backward*.

Farther indicates distance and *further* means to a greater degree or extent.

Use *leaped* instead of *leapt*, and be consistent with other similar words.

Among and *amid* instead of *amongst* and *amidst*.

Gray for the Americans, and *grey* for the English. The letter *a* for the Americans and *e* for the English. You'll never confuse them again.

That That

Revise so you don't repeat the words, as in "He read that that person . . ."

Is/Was/Were

These words weaken a sentence. Compare *she was wearing* to *she wore*. Instead of "Ray was on the boat," substitute *was* with a word or phrase such as *fidgeted, rocked on his heels*, or *paced*. In other words, use an action.

Would You Mind if . . .

If detectives knock on a door and inquire if the resident would mind if they came in to ask some questions, the answer should be "No, come in," not "Yes, come in." Of course, if the character doesn't want to answer questions, but she will despite her annoyance, the answer could be "Yes, but come in anyway."

A Month of Stun Days

If a reader knows her days-per-month data and she reads about a character doing something on September 31, you've sidetracked her. Best-case scenario—she'll shake her head, roll her eyes, and then continue reading.

Worst-case scenario—she'll want to verify the information, but she left her phone at her friend's house. When she asks her husband how many days blah blah blah, he shrugs, and then when she tries to find her calendar . . .

In case you've never learned or have forgotten the mnemonic, memorize the following:

Thirty days hath September, April, June, and November. All the rest have thirty-one except February that has twenty-eight and in leap year, twenty-nine.

If you've been sitting for a while, why not stand and do a rap version of it?

Character Study

There's no rule regarding how many characters should be in a story, but make sure there's a good reason to have each one. Sometimes writers have too many characters, which detract from the main character and cause confusion.

A story that involves some kind of suspense is often more intriguing with fewer characters because the risk factor is greater. However, depending on the length of your story, you could have a few disposable characters. Their function would be to increase the fear factor by their untimely and violent deaths that hint at what might happen to the main character.

Only What the Perspective Character Knows

Resist the urge to write something like this: "If only he had seen the monster's fangs and red eyes as it watched his every move." And don't project things into the future as in the following: "Years later he'd look back on that day and . . ." Read more about this in chapter eleven, "Reader Immersion."

Stuttering, Dialect, Jargon, and Slang

Stuttering, dialect, jargon, and slang can interfere with the pace. With stuttering and dialect, consider subtly referencing that the character either stutters or speaks in dialect. If you feel you must use jargon or uncommon slang, find subtle ways to reveal the meaning, such as pairing the words with an action or having another character's dialogue suggest the meaning.

Beginning Participial Phrases

The following sentence has a beginning participial phrase that modifies the wrong word: Walking across the street, a car hit Raymond. This sentence structure communicates that the car was walking across the street when it hit Raymond. Not only is the mistake a speed bump, but also these types of sentences can create hilarious distracting humor.

Using several consecutive sentences with beginning participial phrases, even without the mistakes, is especially inadvisable.

Mirror, Mirror on the Wall,
What's the Worst Cliché of All?
When someone stares at me and spies
the bags that are beneath his eyes.

They always comment about the bags. And the caveat about this cliché applies to any reflective surface.

Use fresher ideas to reveal appearances, and sprinkle in the details intermittently rather than having a glut of description.

Have another character comment about the protagonist's appearance. Use actions, such as having a tall man duck when he walks through a doorway, showing a man buckling a belt in a different hole to illustrate he's lost weight, or having a woman hold her breath and her stomach in when she zips her skirt.

A character could also look at an old picture and think about how her appearance changed. She might reveal her hair color and length when she brushes strands from her coat sleeves. Maybe she tells someone she wears a certain color to match her eyes.

Foreign Words

These can be confusing speed bumps if the meaning isn't clear from the text.

Names

Don't have characters constantly using people's names in dialogue. It's annoying and not realistic. People usually don't use names in conversations unless there's a reason to, for example, when they're addressing a different person in a conversation or perhaps when they're angry or warning someone about danger.

Battle Rattled

In a fight scene, paragraph each time a different person throws a punch or initiates some other violence. It's difficult to follow the fight if a paragraph contains the actions of both characters, and the conflict loses impact.

Sentence Revision

For tighter prose, try to avoid final prepositional phrases. Doesn't "Gregory broke his leg when he walked to the store" sound crisper as "Gregory, walking to the store, broke his leg." At the end put the sentence's important point. This location gets the most emphasis because of the punctuation mark and the space that create a pause. Which is more important? That Gregory walked to the store or that he broke his leg?

Repetitious Words

Search for the following words, and when possible, revise, remove, or limit them:

- really
- actually

- very
- some
- thought
- look
- -ly (adverbs)
- heard
- mused
- wondered
- felt
- could
- would
- started to
- began to
- had to

Third-person-limited deep point of view removes the necessity of using filters, such as *wondered*, *thought*, or *mused*. For example, instead of writing "He wondered if he should see a movie or go to a concert," revise to "Should he see a movie or go to a concert?"

Everyone has overused words, and it would be worthwhile to add them to the word-search list.

Comments for Improvements

Many of my suggestions for contest entries' improvements involve the following issues:

- unimaginative title
- lagging pace
- poor prose and proofreading
- absent beginning hook
- stilted or unrealistic dialogue
- protagonist without much appeal
- weak plot
- minimal variety in sentence formats as well as paragraph and sentence lengths
- needs more conflict and microtension
- too much narrative and not enough dialogue and action
- confusing transitions between past, present, and future
- requires suspension of disbelief regarding the plot, story details, or the protagonist's behavior
- lack of sensory description

- ending too abrupt or lacking a satisfying sense of resolution

10

Reducing Word Count

Most contests have a maximum word-count rule that writers *must* follow. The limits for flash fiction create special challenges. Don't think you can sneak a few extra words in without someone's discovering the infraction. This chapter presents methods of reducing the word count.

Refer to the previous list of overused words. You can usually eliminate many occurrences of the word *that* and still have an understandable sentence.

Use possessives instead of words and phrases such as *of* and *of the*:

The words of Henry. Henry's words.

The light of the lamp. The lamp's light. Or even better, the lamplight.

Revise wordy sentences. A possible revision for the sentence "Most contests have a maximum word-count rule that writers must follow" is "Most contests have a mandatory maximum word count." The shortened version of "Don't think you can sneak a few extra words in without someone's discovering the infraction" is "Don't think you can sneak in undetected words." The adjectives *mandatory* and *undetected* replaced the phrases "rule that writers must adhere to" and "a few extra words in without someone's discovering the infraction."

Use sentence fragments. Besides smoothing the prose and creating sentence-format variety, they conserve words. Complete sentence: He heard someone scream and run down the block.

Fragment: "A scream and pounding footsteps."

Don't waste words by having your character tell people things your reader already knows. Readers also get antsy with the repetition. If the character has to reveal something to someone else, then convey it to the reader with narrative such as "He told him about Bill's murder."

Delete unnecessary prepositional phrases. Revise "The most interesting scene in the movie had . . ." to this version: "The most interesting scene had . . ." if it's obvious the interesting scene concerns the movie.

Use active voice, which is usually the right choice anyway. "The artist painted the picture," not "The picture was painted by the artist."

Remove unnecessary dialogue tags.

In a conversation, don't have characters using each person's name or have them rarely saying it.

Use hyphenation, but make sure the contest accepts hyphenated words as one word. "The man, who was born in Brazil, now lives in America" becomes "The Brazilian-born man now lives in America."

Revise sentences starting with *there is, there was,* or *there were,* also known as expletives. Change "There was a vampire living in the castle" to "A vampire lived in the castle."

11

Reader Immersion

You've lost sleep and your appetite waiting to hear about that contest entry you submitted four weeks ago. You have a good feeling about it, though. Your title is clever, and the first sentence rocks. The beginning scene is a heart-thumping ride. The dictionary's definition of excellence references your plot. Using a jeweler's magnifier and your lapidary skills, you eliminated all flaws. You're convinced the judge will remember your incisive and resonant finale on his deathbed.

However, when you receive that results email, you learn that your diligent efforts didn't merit effusive praise. The diplomatic comments add up to the editorial equivalent of a shrug and a *meh*.

What went wrong?

Maybe you didn't immerse your reader in the story. Were your descriptions so vivid that the reader could imagine herself in the setting? Did you make the reader care about your characters, especially the protagonist? Was there something or someone the character had strong feelings against?

Next, I'll discuss methods of increasing reader immersion and elements that create the opposite effect.

Point of View

First person point of view fosters a personal look at the protagonist. However, third-person-limited deep point of view is a popular contemporary choice. A third-person protagonist is referred to as he, she, it, or the character's name, instead of the *I* of first person or the *you* of the second person. As I mentioned in the second chapter, the second-person point of view doesn't have universal appeal.

With third-person-limited deep point of view, the limited aspect refers to the reader's experiencing a scene through the perspective of a single character. The deep aspect refers to the avoidance of author intrusion.

Examples of Author Intrusion

- Stating things the perspective character doesn't know. "If only she had seen the murderer staring at her from . . ."
- Having a character on a soapbox to force-feed an agenda. Subtlety is more effective. Instead of telling, show people making bad choices and suffering the consequences.
- Telegraphing—revelation of future events. "Years later, he'd look back on that day . . ."
- Author comments interrupting the text. Parenthetical remarks interfere with the pace. "Kevin went to the bank (though he had no intentions of drawing out the money)." The parentheses aren't necessary. "Kevin went to the bank, though he had no intentions of drawing out the money."

Details the Character Wouldn't Process

The snow had piled up, and she had trouble walking in her long blue-velvet skirt with the embroidered red flowers.

Filtering

Using phrases such as *he felt*, *he knew*, *he wondered*, etc.

Information the Character Wouldn't know Because of Education, Background, etc.

Mark admired how Sally looked in her Ralph Lauren dress.

She felt a sharp pain in her hypothalamus.

Often it's info dumping.

Reaction before Action

She screamed when the man grabbed her.

Maximizing Reader Immersion with Point of View

It's important to understand what third-person-limited deep point of view is and how it can immerse a reader. I'm going to give an example of a third-person story excerpt with head hopping (more than one character's perspective in the scene), and then rewrite the piece with third-person-limited deep point of view to show the reader-immersion difference.

Third-Person Point of View

Greg was trying to decide if he should explore the old house. He believed the stories he'd heard about the murders. And the ghosts. "Maybe going in is too dangerous."

Ariana was so disgusted. He was such a coward, and she'd known he'd lose his nerve.

Greg felt cold. He wrapped his jacket with the broken zipper around him. He could see two cats on the fence. He heard their yowls. He knew they were warning him.

Ariana didn't care if he wouldn't go in. "I don't care if you stay outside. I'll go in alone." She wouldn't have been so brave, though, if she'd known what she'd find there.

Be my guest, Greg thought (even though he doubted she'd survive).

Third-Person-Limited Deep Point of View

The following version only utilizes Greg's perspective:

Should he explore the mansion? The icy gusts stabbed him, and Greg slouched against the front door. Something must have gnawed the gingerbread trim. The moldy remains hanging from the porch roof resembled rotten uneven teeth.

He bit his lip. If the rumors were true, a safe packed with gold bricks would be worth the risk. Some things, though, weren't just tall tales. Like the murders.

What about the ghosts?

Ariana sighed and then scowled. "You're such a coward. I knew you'd lose your nerve."

The freezing wind pummeled him. If only his jacket's zipper hadn't jammed. Greg pulled the jacket tighter around himself. Would his chapped hands freeze?

Two black cats on a gray wooden fence swatted each other, and they yowled warnings. He shuddered. The cats dashed to the mansion, and a shattered basement window swallowed them.

"I'm going in even if you won't." She shoved him aside.

Be my guest, Ariana. "I'll stay alive even if you don't." He fisted his hands. After what she'd done to her brother, she deserved the hellhole's fury.

In the second rendition, I deleted the filtering words, *known, could see, knew,* and *heard.* Without them, the revised sentences have greater impact. The question about the mansion woven into the text is Greg's direct thought and draws the reader in. The first version distances the reader with its explanation (Greg was trying to decide . . .). This version also doesn't head hop, like the first one. In other words, it doesn't reveal what's going on inside both characters' minds. Also Greg's reaction to the cold has greater sensory impact than just stating that he felt cold.

Instead of telling the reader that Ariana was disgusted, her actions of sighing, scowling, and shoving reveal her attitude. The telegraphing about what Ariana would find in a half hour is author intrusion. Don't italicize thoughts unless the perspective character is directly talking to someone in his mind, for example, *Be my guest, Ariana*. In the first example, "he thought" is unnecessary, and the parenthetical comment is author intrusion. The sentence is much smoother without them and with the other changes in the second example.

Words That Pop

Another way to increase reader immersion is to replace anemic nouns and verbs with specific, vivid, and fresh words.

Compare the following two scenes:

Rhonda was mad. "I don't like what you're doing."

Vince said something under his breath and kept watching TV.

She crossed her arms. "I'm talking to you," she said.

He stood. "Well, I'm sick of your nagging."

*

Rhonda glared at him. "How dare you watch football all day! Guess you forgot my birthday *again*."

Vince mumbled, and ramped up the volume.

She stamped her foot. "When I take the floor, you better be all ears, you jock wannabe."

Vince shot up. "Quit badgering me."

Would you Root for Your Main Character?

Ask yourself that question, because if a reader doesn't find the character appealing, the reader's story immersion will decrease.

Some suggestions for making your protagonist irresistible include the following:

- a strong, distinctive voice
- a sense of humor
- kindness to animals, children, or the elderly
- quirkiness or whimsy
- courage, honesty, and nobility
- surmounting a challenge

I can't overemphasize the value of having a protagonist with a strong, distinctive voice. It will immediately grab the reader. Most of my highest-scoring entries have an unforgettable voice.

12

Endings

Few things are as frustrating as reading a story that appears to have all the right ingredients, but the ending is a letdown. What makes a great finale?

Let's first start with endings that aren't great.

The Cavalry Ending

It's much more satisfying for a reader to get involved with the protagonist and have the protagonist experience a conflict and then somehow work out the situation. What's not satisfying is when someone else "rescues" the protagonist, and it's particularly ill advised if the "cavalry" lacks an earlier reference.

It Was All a Dream

An it-was-all-a-dream ending worked for *The Wizard of Oz*, but I would think twice before using it for a contest entry. Readers usually feel cheated by this finale.

The Trailing Ending

Another problematic ending is the trailing ending. The writer doesn't realize the right place to stop and continues for several sentences, resulting in an ending without impact.

The inner-monologue ending is a type of trailing ending. This ending involves a character summing up the story and droning on and on.

Another type of trailing ending is when a character commits suicide, but afterwards, though dead, engages in maudlin reflection.

Sometimes the character already used the knife, drank the poison, shot the bullet, etc. However, while waiting for the inevitable, she engages in a conversation with absent or present people. These ramblings are often full of purple prose, venom, and histrionics.

Sometimes they continue for several pages.

Is a Page Missing?

An additional unsatisfying ending is one that's too abrupt, which leaves the story with an unfinished quality. The finale doesn't seem smooth. The author doesn't tie up the ends.

Some of these endings don't seem like endings at all, and it's always a bad sign when a judge tries to read the next page, but there is no next page.

13

Contest-Winning Components

It's intriguing when I start to read a story and recognize a possible winner. The ability to elicit this immediate response is in a writer's favor because it affects the story's general impression.

Probably the most important elements that trigger this assessment are the initial hook, the protagonist's strong voice, and the excellent prose. Well-written sentences don't meander with unnecessary phrases and clauses. Well-written sentences don't confuse readers. Well-written sentences help prevent a lagging pace.

You will still have to perform well throughout the plot and resolution, but if the start reflects high quality, the likelihood is that that you will immerse the judge in the story, which may color his overall reaction.

Contestants don't realize how many stories most judges have read. In the introduction I stated that I've read thousands. Freshness and creativity are assets. But some elements are ubiquitous, such as the previously mentioned mirror scene, where the character describes his appearance. Another cliché is the restaurant conversation. Instead, choose an unusual setting that provides built-in tension, which adds interest. And adding conflict can elevate a scene from one that just reveals information to something that evokes intrigue.

I analyzed one of the contests I judged to assess the major positive comments in high-ranking stories. The comments referenced items such as creative use of prompts, vivid descriptions that use all five senses, attention-getting titles, endings that show good resolution, and imaginative figurative language.

I also had favorable things to say about exotic or unusual settings, which generate intrigue and provide opportunities for rich sensory description. Often these stories have a protagonist who is an outsider, which creates the possibility of culture clash and the suspense and pace enhancement generated by conflict.

And speaking of conflict, use more than one source by including both macrotension (the main source) and microtension (exacerbating factors). For example, if someone is following the main character, have the protagonist also suffering from a cold, worrying about her vehicle breaking down, and hearing a storm prediction on the radio. Microtension can maintain and heighten the suspense.

I hope the suggestions in this book and your own particular applications of them result in successful contest entries.

.

14

Checklist

You think you've covered all the elements, and you have a story that's a sure winner. Before you submit your manuscript, check your entry for the following items:

- an entry conforming to the judge's or contest-sponsor's preferences
- attention-getting title
- a hook first sentence
- protagonist introduction, empathy building, brief mention of setting, and genre disclosure included optimally in the first paragraph or at least on the first page

- characters' names not starting with the same letters or having other similarities
- specific nouns and verbs rather than description with adjectives and adverbs
- word search for -ly adverbs
- no omitted words or quotation marks
- no unintentional word repetition
- possible revision of end-of-sentence prepositional phrases
- no head hopping
- variety in sentence and paragraph lengths
- correct spelling of words such as *its* and *it's* and *discreet* and *discrete*
- no unnecessary use of the word *that*
- possible revision of sentences with *is*, *are*, or *was* occurrences
- unless otherwise indicated, a beginning, middle, and end and not a vignette
- avoidance of unnecessary use of the word *said*, sometimes by using beats or by eliminating the dialogue tag
- proofreading
- final reading of content and formatting requirements for adherence guarantee

 Patricia La Barbera, MFA, is an author and an editor who specializes in genre categories. She also teaches writing and judges contests. Various journals and anthologies have published her short stories and poetry. She organized the Sarasota Editors Association and SRQ Horror, Science Fiction, and Fantasy Writers. Patricia La Barbera is a member of the Catholic Writers Guild, the Editorial Freelancers Association, Mystery Writers of America, and an active member of the Horror Writers Association. She lives in Florida with her husband. Visit www.patricialabarbera.com for more information, or contact her at editor@patricialabarbera.com.

Other Books by the Author

Genre Writing

Castle Wolves

The Wolf's Enemy

Wolf Cult

The Celtic Crow Murders

Humorous Horror Poetry